AF753452

FUN AND GAMES

Bubbles

Addition and Subtraction

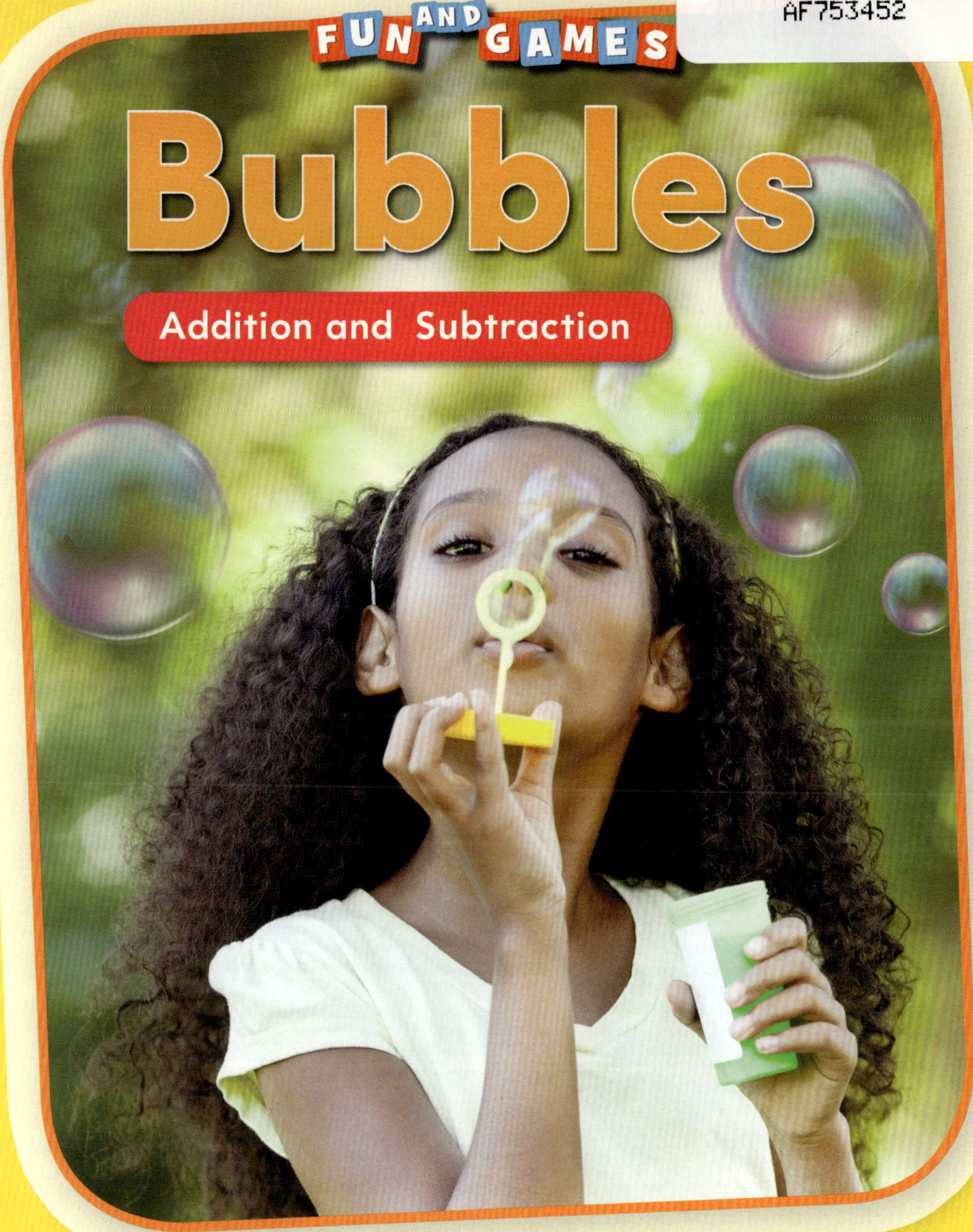

Logan Avery

1, 2, 3 bubbles

4, 5, 6 bubbles

7, 8, 9 bubbles

9, 8, 7 bubbles

6, 5, 4 bubbles

3, 2, 1 bubble

So many bubbles!

Problem Solving

Friends are blowing bubbles. Use objects or pictures to solve the problems. Then, match the math facts to your work.

1. Kim blew 3 bubbles. She blows 2 more. How many bubbles does she blow?

2. Sal blew 3 bubbles. Then, 2 popped. How many bubbles are left?

A. $3 + 2 = \square$ **B.** $3 - 2 = \square$

Answer Key

1. 5 bubbles; A

2. 1 bubble; B

Consultants

Nicole Belasco, M.Ed.
Kindergarten Teacher, Colonial School District

Colleen Pollitt, M.A.Ed.
Math Support Teacher, Howard County Public Schools

Publishing Credits

Rachelle Cracchiolo, M.S.Ed., *Publisher*
Conni Medina, M.A.Ed., *Managing Editor*
Dona Herweck Rice, *Series Developer*
Emily R. Smith, M.A.Ed., *Series Developer*
Diana Kenney, M.A.Ed., NBCT, *Content Director*
June Kikuchi, *Content Director*
Véronique Bos, *Creative Director*
Robin Erickson, *Art Director*
Stacy Monsman, M.A., and Karen Malaska, M.Ed., *Editors*
Michelle Jovin, M.A., *Associate Editor*
Fabiola Sepulveda, *Graphic Designer*

Image Credits: All images from iStock and/or Shutterstock.

Library of Congress Cataloging-in-Publication Data

Names: Avery, Logan, author.
Title: Fun and games : bubbles / Logan Avery.
Other titles: Bubbles
Description: Huntington Beach, CA : Teacher Created Materials, [2018] | Audience: K to grade 3.
Identifiers: LCCN 2017059900 (print) | LCCN 2018016937 (ebook) | ISBN 9781480759602 (e-book) | ISBN 9781425856229 (pbk.)
Subjects: LCSH: Counting--Juvenile literature. | Bubbles--Juvenile literature.
Classification: LCC QA113 (ebook) | LCC QA113 .A9425 2018 (print) | DDC 513.2/11--dc23
LC record available at https://lccn.loc.gov/2017059900

Teacher Created Materials
5301 Oceanus Drive
Huntington Beach, CA 92649-1030
www.tcmpub.com

ISBN 978-1-4258-5622-9
© 2019 Teacher Created Materials, Inc.
Printed by 51250
PO 16300 / Printed in USA

Math Talk

1. How do you know when to add or subtract?

2. How can knowing $2 + 2 = 4$ help you solve $4 - 2 = \square$?

6 + 2 = ? 8 − 2 = ?

FUN AND GAMES

Bubbles

Addition and Subtraction

There are bubbles, bubbles everywhere! How many can you add and subtract?

Teacher Created Materials PUBLISHING

Reading Levels
Lexile®: NP
Guided Reading: LB

Operations and Algebraic Reasoning

ISBN: 978-1-4258-5622-9
50000
9 781425 856229
27273

$18 - 3 = \square$

Art and Culture

Diwali

Addition and Subtraction

Joseph Otterman